Ackerberg House & Addition

THE MONACELLI PRESS

Ackerberg House & Addition

Richard Meier

Design Team	Richard Meier
	Michael Palladino
	Gunter Standke
Collaborators	Paul Mitchell
	Marc Hacker
	Brian Healy
	Hans Li
	Mark Mascheroni
	Daniel Stuver
	Steven Theodore

First published in the United States of America in 1996 by
The Monacelli Press, Inc.,
10 East 92nd Street, New York, New York 10128.

Library of Congress Cataloging-in-Publication Data
Ackerberg House & addition : Richard Meier.
p.   cm. — (One house)
Includes bibliographical references.
ISBN 1-885254-27-X (pbk.)
1. Ackerberg House (Malibu, Calif.) 2. Architecture, Postmodern—California—Malibu.
3. Malibu (Calif.)—Buildings, structures, etc. I. Meier, Richard, 1934– . II. Series.
NA7238.M26A34   1996
728'.372'0979493—dc20   96-5627

Printed and bound in Italy

Designed and composed by *Group* **C** Inc New Haven/Boston

Ackerberg Contents

Introduction

Richard Meier

I first met Norman and Lisette Ackerberg in Los Angeles at the time I was being interviewed as architect for the Getty Center. Their house on the beach in Malibu was my first completed work in Southern California; the Getty, which began at about the same time, is still under construction. The Ackerberg House was an important exploration of building for the gentle climate and strong sunlight of the Los Angeles basin.

The site was at once fantastic and flawed. Beachfront property off the Pacific Coast Highway, it had views of both the nearby range of mountains across the highway and the wide expanse of the Pacific Ocean. It was, however, a relatively narrow site with neighboring houses in extremely close proximity on either side. Norman and Lisette were seeking to build something simple and uncontrived. I began with the cultural and natural inspirations of the region.

By referring to both the indigenous courtyard types and modern architecture of Southern California, their qualities of light and interplay of vertical and horizontal planes, I designed the Ackerberg House to mediate between the contextual extremes of the mountains and the ocean. U-shaped in plan, the house encloses a courtyard which extends the living space of the interior to a larger exterior "room" and beyond. The house's visual sense of expansion is limited only by the horizon.

From the Pacific Coast Highway, the house reads as a layered wall of rectilinear sheets, while from the terrace and pool it is experienced as a dense massing of white posts and curved sunscreens. Progression through the house begins at the highway side, the north facade, which is clad in white ceramic tile. From a double-height exterior entrance hall, one passes through a loggia along the periphery of the courtyard, from which views of the Pacific are framed by the wings of the house. The courtyard, with its high walls and the undulating, stuccoed surface of the living room wall, interprets the experience of the mountains on a domestic scale. Entry into the public area of the house occurs past the curved wall of the living area, at the actual front door.

The living room is the center of the house, a dramatic double-height space with clerestory windows and sliding glass doors. In order to modulate and inflect the intense California light, the house is generously provided with brise-soleils. These sun-screens, vertical surfaces pulled away from the mass of the house at roof level, create a transitional space between the house and the terrace, a three-dimensional facade which can be occupied.

Six years after the house was completed, in 1992, the Ackerbergs contacted me again to say that they required additional space in Malibu. My initial response was to discourage the idea of adding on; the house was, to my mind, complete. With trepidation I considered the formal and programmatic possibilities of the extension. It was difficult because a certain scale and set of proportions had been established. Once the decision had been made, however, my goal became to make the house even better than it was in its original incarnation.

I thought the addition should continue to explore the idea of spatial progression and should allow its occupants to step outside, onto a terrace or balcony, from every room. I realized that the only place to put the addition was in front as a third story of 1,200 square feet above the guest wing. Among the constraints influencing this choice were local height limitations. The program for this third story included an exercise room, artist's studio, and bath.

On the highway side, the addition was set back to minimize its mass. The visible portions actually improved the house from the street, rendering it more noticeable. On the ocean side, a pier anchors the enlarged wing, and a stair from the courtyard slides behind the pier to form a small third-story terrace. The balcony extension articulates and animates its corner.

To set the new level unobtrusively into the existing structure, detailing was kept identical to the original, and steel railings were extended to lace it together. Some structural upgrading was necessary to reinforce second-story walls that had been designed to support only a roof.

The massing of the guest wing evolves from opaque garages at ground level to lighter guest quarters at mid-level to lightest addition at top. This intention was reiterated by a glass walkway on the addition level which projects complex light and shadow plays onto the second-floor guest quarters. I tried to design railings and walkways at this level that would, like the bridge of a ship, give the feeling of heading out to sea.

Even with the addition, the basic organization of the Ackerberg House remains intact. The object quality of the pavilion and its more public living-dining-library wing were not affected by the changes to the more private wing. On the contrary, the house has improved due to the more recent architectural intervention, as well as to the maturing of its landscaping, which is certainly a part of the architecture. The hedge along the courtyard, having grown as the house has grown, completes the outdoor "room." In the courtyard, with its view of the endless Pacific, the house, sky, and mountains have become elements in a spatial conception that locates the occupant at the junction of nature and architecture.

Before designing this addition, I believed my residential architecture was best preserved in its state of initial design and construction. As a result of my experience with the Ackerberg House I now believe that, with the proper attitude, it is possible to change a house for the better and to infuse it with new life.

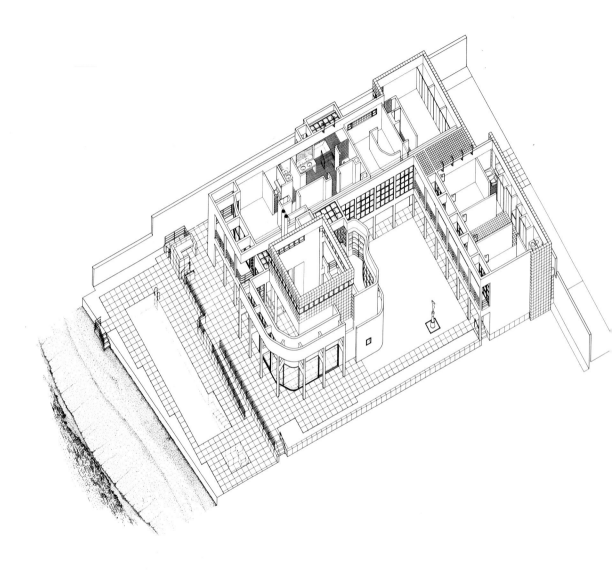

axonometric before addition

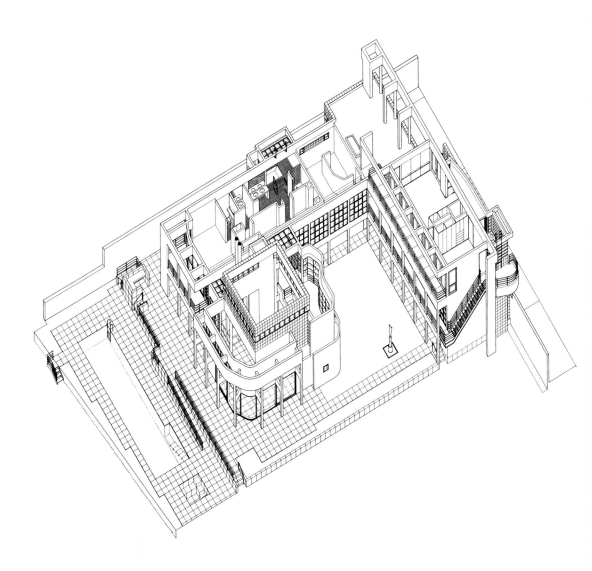

axonometric after addition

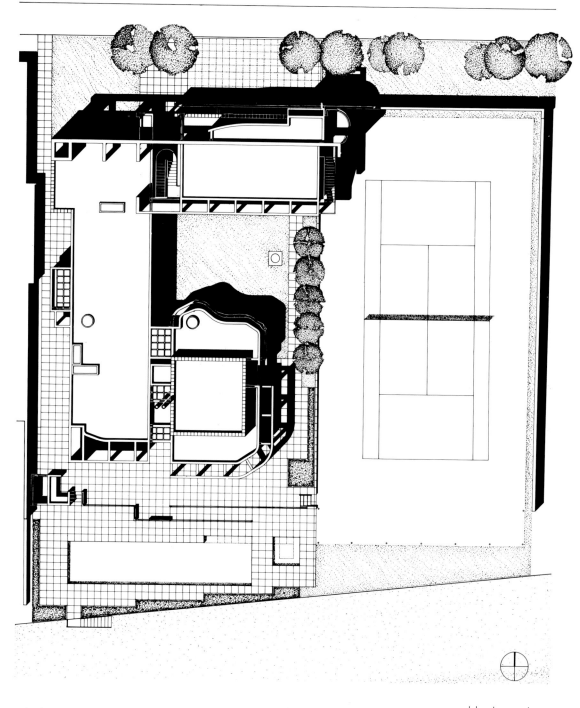

site plan

|2 |5 |10|

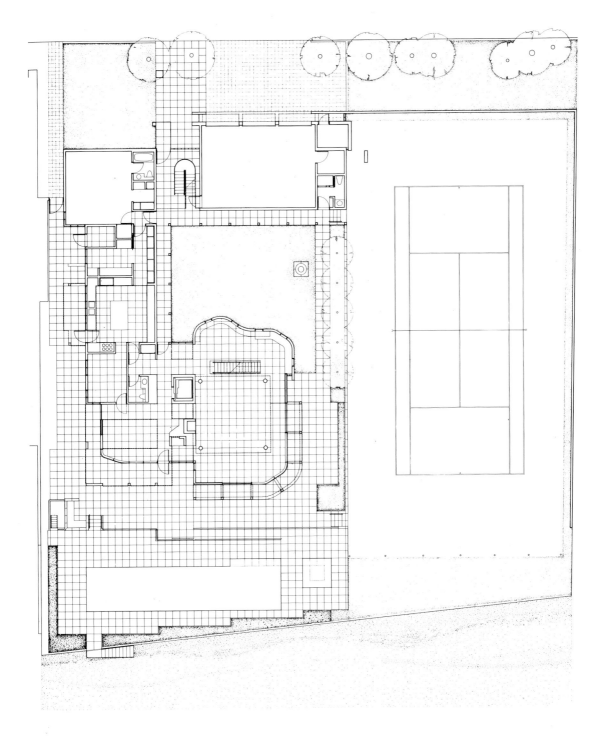

first level plan

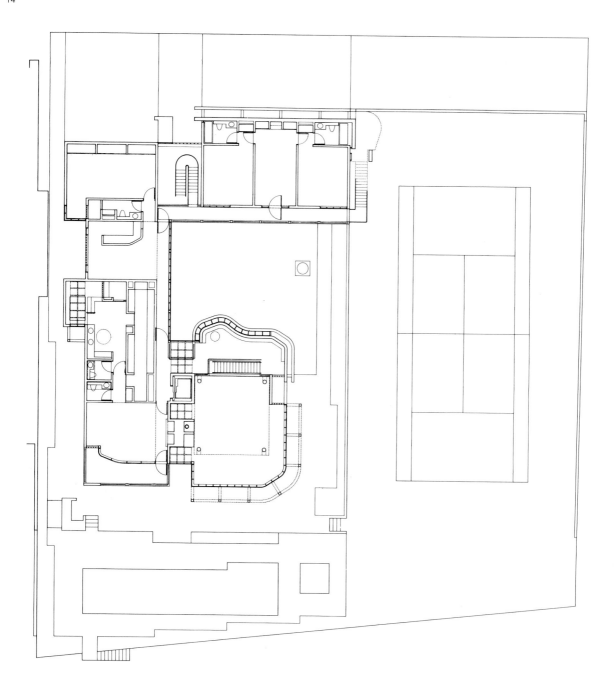

second level plan

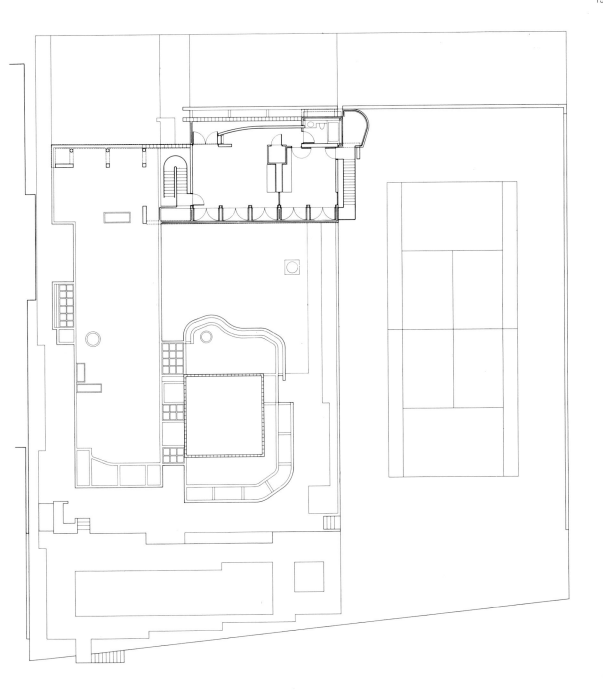

third level plan

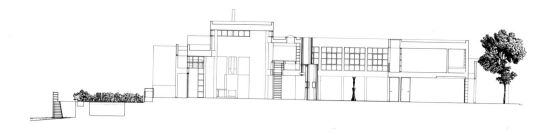

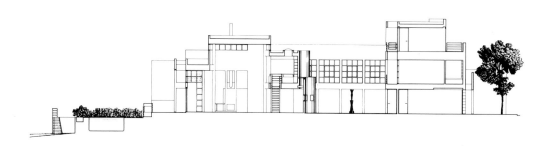

longitudinal section before (top) and after (bottom) addition

cross section before (top) and after (bottom) addition

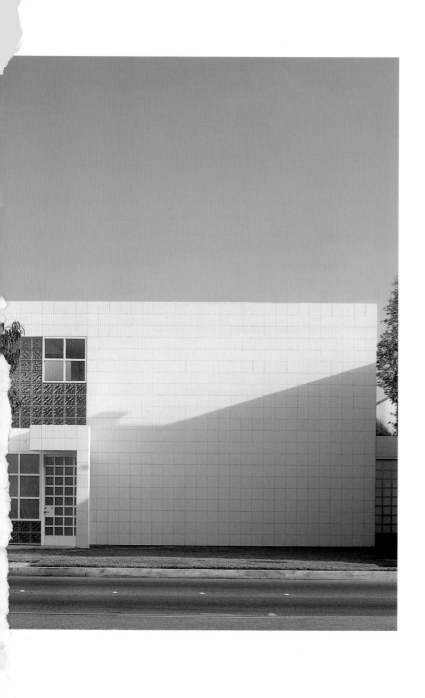

1 north facade before addition

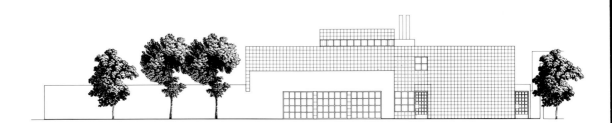

north elevation before addition

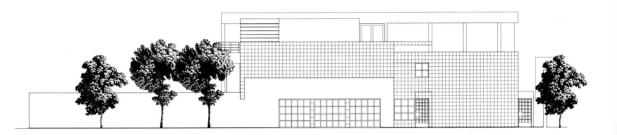

north elevation after addition

2 north facade after addition

1
2

3
4

3 entry before addition **4** entry after addition

7, 8 view from vestibule to courtyard before (above) and after (right) addition

9,10,11 courtyard and living room wall

13, 14, 15 living and dining areas

16 living room

17 living room (overleaf)

18, 19 views of the balcony overlooking the living room

20 view of the living room from the balcony

21, 22 south facade (first and second overleaf)

23,24 south facade at dusk and at night

23
24

25 terraces on south facade **26** view from the terrace to the Pacific

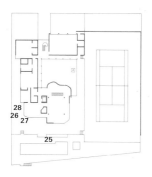

28
26
27
25

27,28 terrace under brise-soleils

29, 30 south facade with brise-soleils **31** poolside detailing (overleaf)

32 brise-soleils **33** view to guest wing before addition

34 south facade with guest wing before addition

36 guest wing before addition

37 guest wing after addition

38, 39, 40 views to the Pacific from the poolside terrace

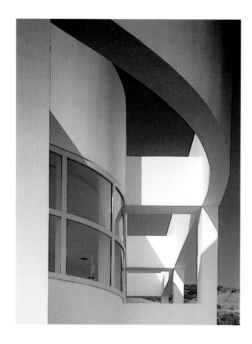

41 detail of brise-soleils **42** view along the east facade to the Pacific **43** east facade (overleaf)

44

45

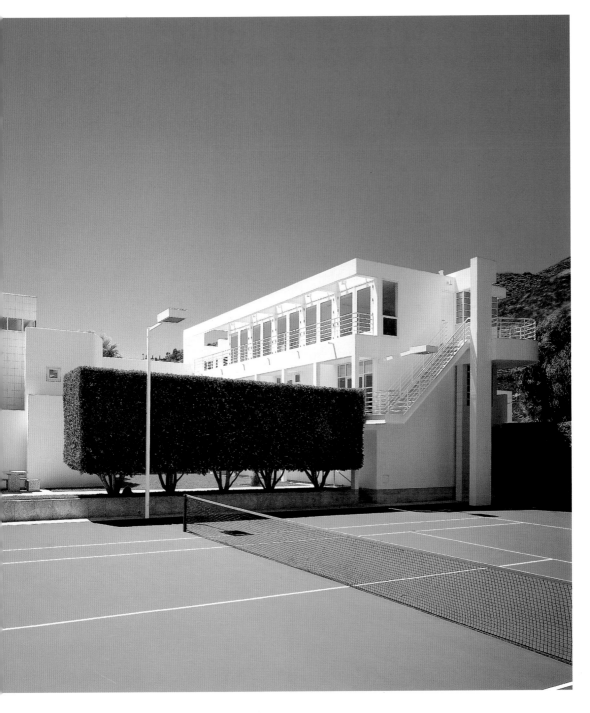

44,45 east elevation and courtyard from the tennis court before and after addition

Bibliography

Betsky, Aaron. "Beach House Masterfully Mixes Sense of Structure and Freedom." *Los Angeles Times*, Mar. 7, 1991, J2.

Contal, Marie-Hélène. "Meier à Malibu." *Architecture Intérieure Créé*, Feb.-Mar. 1989, 92–97.

Dungen, Mabel van den. "Richard Meier." *Avant Garde*, Oct. 1990, 120–25.

Futagawa, Yukio, ed. "Ackerberg House." *GA Houses*, Dec. 1987, 6–21.

Graaf, Vera. "Luxusdampfer am Strand." *Arckitektur & Wohnen*, June-July 1990, 22–28.

Hollenstein, Roman. "Eine Hymne an Südkaliforniens Licht." *NZZ Folio*, Feb. 1992, 62–63.

Hubeli, Ernst. "Unsichtbare Konstruktion als Allegorie." *Werk, Bauen + Wohnen*, Dec. 1988, 9–11.

Hughes, Robert. "Architecture: Richard Meier." *Architectural Digest*, Oct. 1987, 152–59.

Meier, Richard. "Ackerberg House." *Richard Meier: Architect.* Vol. 2 (1985–91). New York: Rizzoli, 1991, 48–67.

Mulard, Claudine. "La Maison Blanche." *Maison & Jardin*, Mar. 1991, 132–39.

Nakamura, Toshio, ed. "Ackerberg House." *A+U*, Mar. 1988, 34–53.

Papadakis, Andreas C., ed. "Richard Meier, Ackerberg House, Malibu, 1984–86." *Architectural Design*, vol. 58, no. 7–8 (1988), 24–33.

Prichett, Jack. "Richard Meier's Ackerberg House: Beauty at the Beach." *Inside*, Feb.-Mar. 1990, 5–13.

Rykwert, Joseph. "Richard Meier: Two New Houses in USA." *Domus*, Mar. 1987, 29–45.

Stephens, Suzanne. "Malibu Modernism." *Progressive Architecture*, Dec. 1987, 94–101.

Uthmann, Jorg von. "Das weltliche Kloster van Malibu." *Frankfurter Allgemeine Zeitung*, Oct. 29, 1991.

Webb, Michael. "Second Act in Malibu." *Architectural Digest*, Jan. 1995, 144–49, 182.

Photography Credits